IT'S FUN TO LEARN ABOUT
ANIMALS

Claire Llewellyn
Consultant: Michael Chinery

ARMADILLO

NOTES

This book takes a straightforward look at animals, from the way they move and the sounds they make to an exploration of their curious habits and characteristics. Informative text, lively photographs and plenty of activities ensure that children have fun while they learn.

Reading together

Children like to share books. You can help your child by reading aloud the text that accompanies the pictures. Do not expect them to read the book all at once. Go through the book at your child's pace. Look at a couple of pages at a time, and allow a few days for the information to sink in. This way, reading time will always be enjoyable.

Talking it through

Expand your child's understanding of animals by talking about the pictures in the book. Looking through the window, walking in the park and watching television also provide opportunities to talk about animals.

Answering questions

Ask your child questions, and encourage answers. Do not worry if the answers are wrong – making mistakes is part of the learning process. What is important is that your child is willing to try.

Checking your child's understanding

Reinforce your child's understanding about animals by asking useful questions such as – Why do animals have thick fur coats? How can stripes be useful? Which animals swim in the sea?

Learning by doing

The activities have been designed to be easy and fun, with little preparation required. They will also help your child to understand that it really is fun to learn!

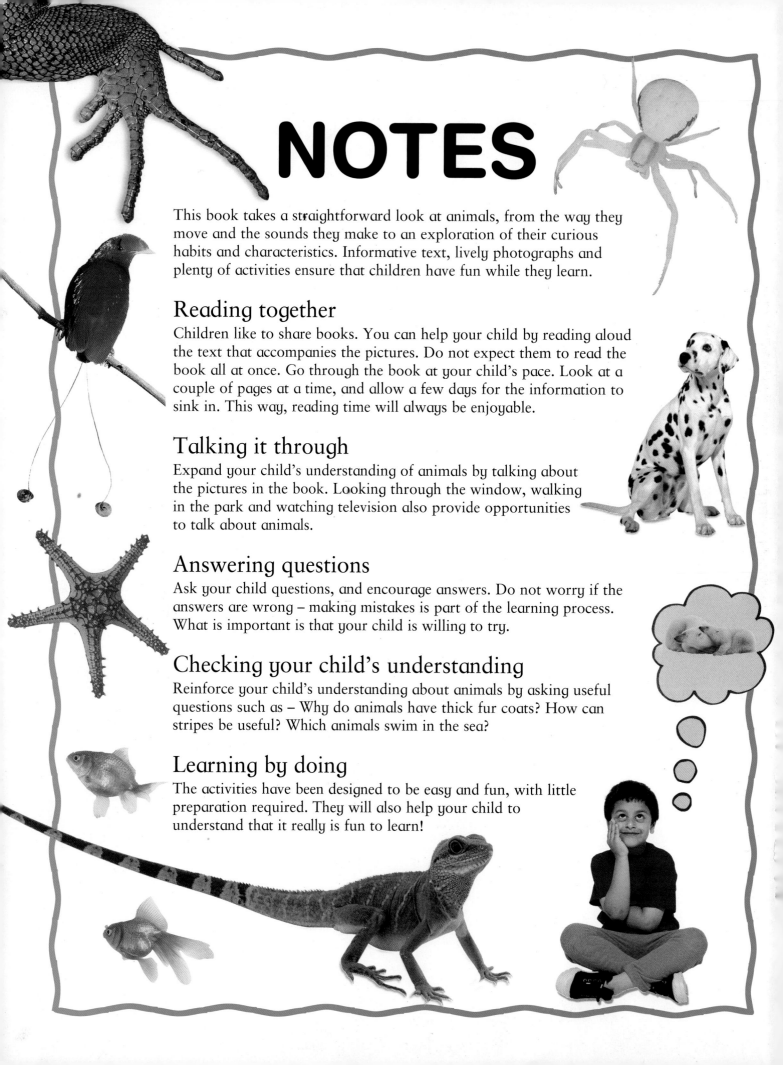

CONTENTS

Furry friends

Some animals have thick, soft fur to keep them warm. Others have hair or feathers that look like fur.

Hold on tight!

Long, skinny fingers help this raccoon to keep a tight grip.

Watch orang-utans swing through the trees – they do it with such ease!

These furry caterpillars will turn into moths.

Wolves howl loudly to one another to stay in touch.

Aroooo!

The tiny feathers on an ostrich's head look like fur!

It's easy for a squirrel to leap from tree to tree – its long, bushy tail keeps it balanced.

Try this!

Play the memory game

1. Think of all the furry animals you've seen at the zoo.

2. Start the game by saying, "I went to the zoo and I saw a polar bear."

3. The next person repeats this and adds another furry animal.

4. Take it in turns to repeat the sentence, adding another furry animal at each turn.

Thick, white fur coats keep these polar bears warm...

...as they snuggle up on the icy Arctic floor.

Tree kangaroos aren't like other kangaroos. They live up in the trees.

A red panda curls up for a snooze in the afternoon sun.

Fabulous feathers

Only one group of animals in the world has feathers. What is it? Yes, you've guessed it – birds!

A pigeon takes off with a ... flap, flap, flap.

Bzzz Bzzz

Here comes a bee! Where? Which way? Two hungry bee-eaters wait for lunch.

Bbbrrrrrr! Bbbrrrrrr!

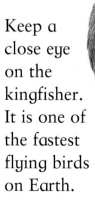

Did you know?

There are over 25,000 feathers on a single swan!

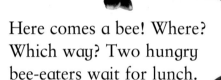

Emperor penguins live in freezing, frosty Antarctica. Layers of thick feathers protect them against biting cold winds.

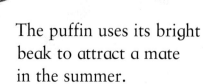

The puffin uses its bright beak to attract a mate in the summer.

Keep a close eye on the kingfisher. It is one of the fastest flying birds on Earth.

Try this!

Make a wrinkly elephant

1. Draw a picture of an elephant and its tail. Cut them out.

2. Draw an eye. Glue on scrunched up pieces of tissue.

3. Attach the tail with a paper fastener, so that it swings.

The marabou stork does not have a voice box. It talks by making a hissing noise.

Hsss! Hsss!

When the giant tortoise feels frightened, it hides its long, flexible neck inside its solid shell.

The wildebeest keeps its head up and its beady eyes open, watching out for lions.

The Komodo dragon is the biggest lizard in the world.

The manatee pulls up plants from the river bed with its large, wrinkly snout.

Sssssssscaly

Scales give animals a tough top coat that protects them from wear and tear.

A chameleon's long, scaly tail curls around and around.

Try this!

Make a tropical fish

1. Draw the outline of an exotic fish on a piece of paper.

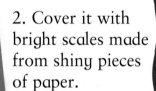

2. Cover it with bright scales made from shiny pieces of paper.

3. Give it an eye and draw on some waves and bubbles.

The scales on this parrot fish shimmer and shine in the light.

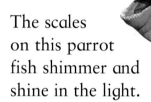

The tortoise needs strong legs to support its heavy shell.

Armadillos are covered in a strong, protective suit of scales.

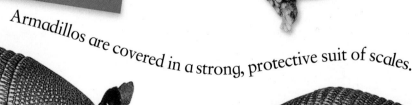

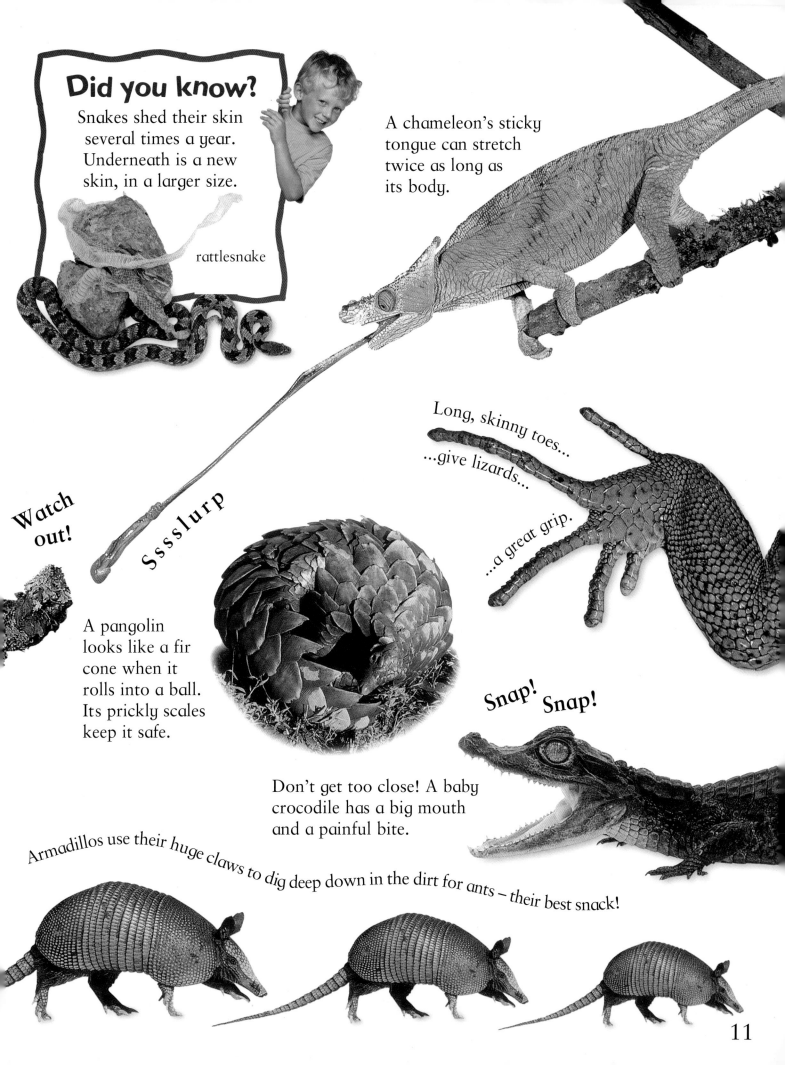

A chameleon's sticky tongue can stretch twice as long as its body.

Watch out!

Sssslurp

A pangolin looks like a fir cone when it rolls into a ball. Its prickly scales keep it safe.

Long, skinny toes...

...give lizards...

...a great grip.

Snap! Snap!

Don't get too close! A baby crocodile has a big mouth and a painful bite.

Armadillos use their huge claws to dig deep down in the dirt for ants – their best snack!

Seeing spots

All sorts of animals are covered in spots. On some animals, the spots fade as the animal grows older.

A white-tailed deer fawn keeps its spots for two months. They help it to hide on the forest floor.

A snow leopard cub has a spotted coat, which hides it in the rocks and snow.

A ladybug's hard, shiny wing-cases have spots on them and protect its delicate wings.

These cheetah cubs will live with their mother until they are about a year and a half old. She teaches them how to stalk and catch their prey.

Try this!

Paint a butterfly picture

1. Paint half a butterfly on paper or card.

2. While the paint is wet, fold the paper, press hard and open it again. Do you have a perfect butterfly?

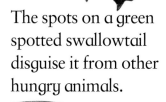

The spots on a green spotted swallowtail disguise it from other hungry animals.

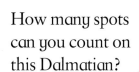

How many spots can you count on this Dalmatian?

These spotty, orange starfish are the size of dinner plates.

SSSSSSSS!

The rainbow boa glows a different shade with every little movement.

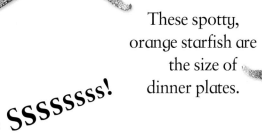

Geckos have no eyelids. They lick their eyes to keep them clean.

13

Simply stripy

Stripes stand out against this white page, but can be a clever disguise against trees, grass or leaves.

A Siberian tiger's stripes help it to hide as it silently stalks through the long grass.

Water dragons shed their skin, but they never lose their stripes!

A snail's shell is its mobile home. It goes wherever the snail goes.

The bright stripes on these caterpillars warn birds that they are not a tasty meal.

There is safety in numbers! Zebras travel in large herds for protection.

Over here!

One...

two...

...three African striped mice.

Ring-tailed lemurs signal to each other with their tails.

What is one way to tell that the copperhead is a poisonous snake? Its bright red and orange stripes are a warning sign.

The zebra butterfly is named after another stripy animal – can you find it on this page?

The okapi is a shy animal that does not like to be noticed. Its stripes help it to hide in the forest.

When attacked, zebras run in different directions to confuse their attacker.

Daringly dazzling

Stunning brightness and interesting patterns make these animals the stars of the natural world.

Aren't I gorgeous?

Sssurprise!

The king bird of paradise sits on its throne, hoping to impress an admirer.

The green tree boa hides high in the trees. It drops on animals that pass below.

Bright yellow crab spiders hide on vivid yellow flowers.

Blue and yellow macaws stand out brightly in the dark rainforest.

Stay away!

This arrow poison frog's startling blue skin is a warning to hungry animals.

The blue morpho butterfly flutters from flower to flower, drinking sweet nectar.

The golden lion tamarin got its name because of its beautiful golden mane.

How does a tree frog balance on a stem? It has sticky suckers on its toes.

Golden beetles shine brightly in the sun, dazzling their enemies away.

The toucan's long, pointy bill is not as heavy as it looks. It is perfect for...

...picking fruit from branches.

Creepy-crawlies

Bugs live all around us. Some of them are living in your home or garden. Look for them under pots, stones or leaves.

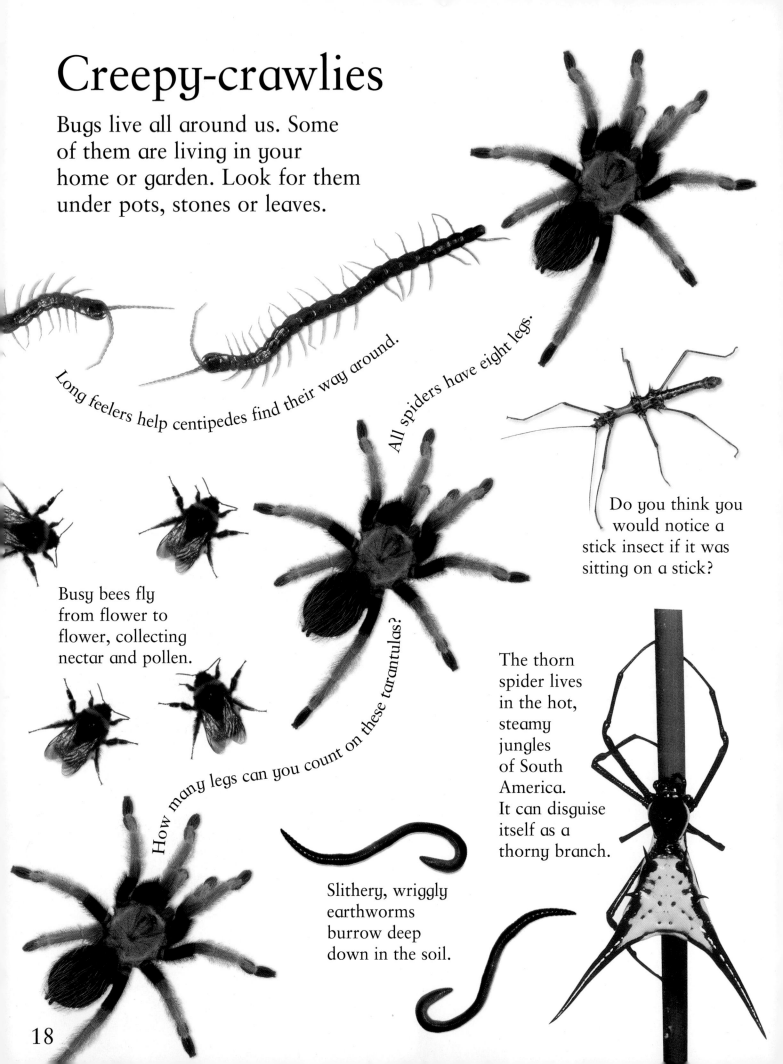

Long feelers help centipedes find their way around.

All spiders have eight legs.

Do you think you would notice a stick insect if it was sitting on a stick?

Busy bees fly from flower to flower, collecting nectar and pollen.

How many legs can you count on these tarantulas?

The thorn spider lives in the hot, steamy jungles of South America. It can disguise itself as a thorny branch.

Slithery, wriggly earthworms burrow deep down in the soil.

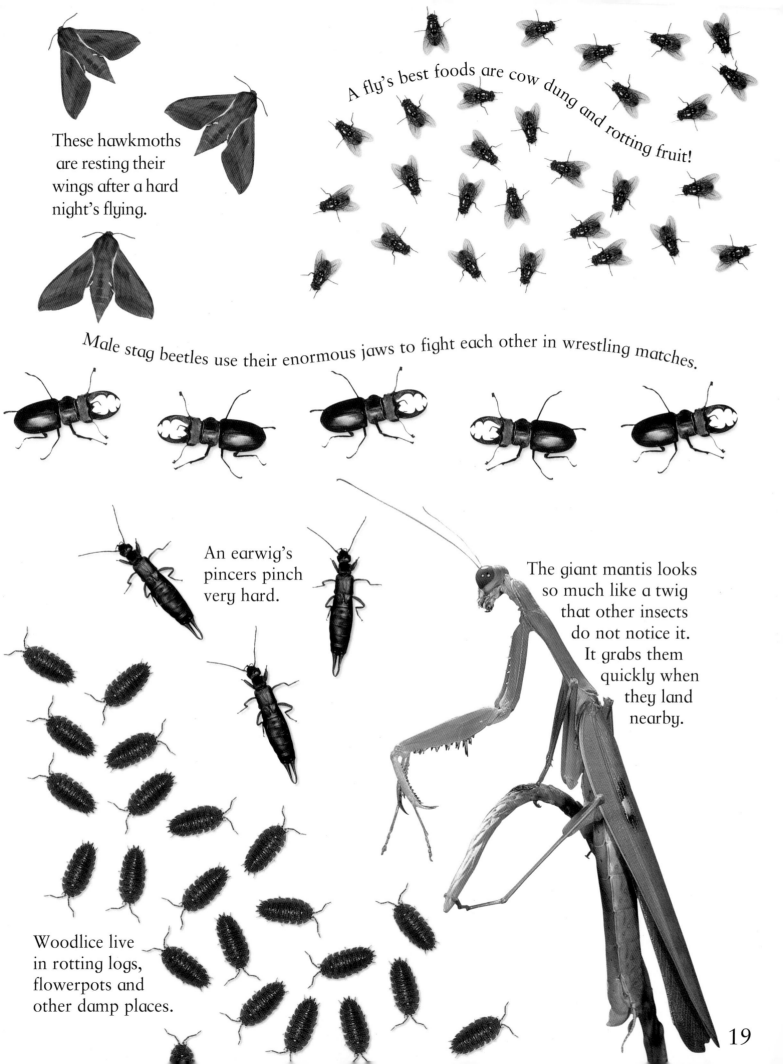

These hawkmoths are resting their wings after a hard night's flying.

A fly's best foods are cow dung and rotting fruit!

Male stag beetles use their enormous jaws to fight each other in wrestling matches.

An earwig's pincers pinch very hard.

The giant mantis looks so much like a twig that other insects do not notice it. It grabs them quickly when they land nearby.

Woodlice live in rotting logs, flowerpots and other damp places.

Fast and fierce

Quick! Run! These wild animals are warning us to stay away. They have sharp teeth and a nasty bite.

The moray eel lurks in underwater caves.

It darts out quickly to catch its prey.

Grrrr!

Grrrr!

Grrrr!

The gruff brown bear has a loud growl. This one is ready for a fight.

Yaruuu!

Yaruuu!

A gorilla's loud, screeching yell warns others to stay away.

Thick, leathery skin, huge jaws and massive teeth – what a frightening sight the crocodile is!

The cheetah is the fastest running animal on Earth. Its speed helps it catch its prey.

Look at the size of this lion's teeth! Other animals keep well away from him.

Rrroar!

In the dark

Imagine you are out in the dark night. Which animals can you hear? Whose eyes are shining in the dark?

The loris has eyes like saucers.

They help it to see in the dark.

Sniff!

Prickly hedgehogs are shy animals. They come out at night for breakfast!

Sniff!

Try this!

Make a night scene

1. Cut out some bushes and trees. Stick them on a piece of black paper.

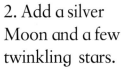

2. Add a silver Moon and a few twinkling stars.

3. Now add some eyes to shine in the dark. Which animal is hiding there?

Insects and worms are the kiwi's food of choice. It sticks its beak into the soil to sniff and smell them out.

Whooo!

Whooo!

Two barn owls take off for a night's hunting.

The flying fox is a bat that feeds on forest fruit at night. It sleeps upside down during the day.

Looking for a tasty dinner? Foxes visit parks and gardens, searching in garbage cans for food.

Badgers live in burrows underground. They come out at night to eat.

The mole lives in dark tunnels underground. It rarely sees the light of day.

The kakapo is a parrot that cannot fly. It crawls around at night.

23

Underwater

The ocean is home to many wonderful creatures that we rarely have a chance to see.

This beluga whale is curious about life above the sea.

Try this!

Underwater scene

1. To make some waves, cut two strips from tissue paper. Glue them at the top of a piece of blue paper.

2. Draw plants and rocks on the bottom of the paper. Glue on some shells. This is the seabed.

3. Draw in the creatures that live in your undersea kingdom.

The green sea turtle uses its paddles to push itself through the water.

The dainty European seahorse is actually no bigger than your hand!

Count the arms on these starfish. How many do they have?

Dolphins are playful animals that love to leap.

Splash!

Splish!

Beware!

When puffer fish feel threatened, they blow up into spiky balls.

Don't touch!

How many tentacles does an octopus have?

Crabs don't walk forwards; they scuttle sideways instead.

Grouper fish are covered with spots so that they blend into the coral reef.

25

Beautiful babies

Baby animals grow up quickly.
They learn to copy what their
parents do.

Baby bats are usually carried on their mother's tummy.

These bear cubs are looking for their mother.
She's always somewhere close by.

Woof!

Woof!

This perky puppy
wants to play.

A seal pup is born on the
ice. Its white furry coat
keeps it warm and hides
it against the snow.

Cheep!

Cheep!

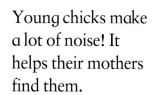

Young chicks make
a lot of noise! It
helps their mothers
find them.

Try this!

Can you find this
koala's baby on the
next page? Look
through this section
of the book and try to
find parents for some
of the other babies, too.

This baby lynx is learning to walk along a branch. It is holding on tightly with its claws.

Baby gorillas are curious creatures.

An albatross chick is an only child.

One day these ostrich chicks will grow into the biggest birds in the world.

Lion cubs are born with spotty coats which hide them in fields of long, dry grass.

A baby koala clings to its mother's back as she climbs through the trees.

Perfect pets

Many people's pets are their best friends. Do you have a pet at home? Can you find it on this page?

Mice have long, sensitive whiskers to help them feel things.

Squeak!

Budgies use their beaks to clean their feathers.

Squeak!

This long-eared rabbit is washing its face with its paws.

Hamsters nibble nuts and seeds. They gnaw at their cages, too!

Cats like to groom themselves after a meal.

The guinea pig has a thick coat of long hair.

Gerbils are busy little animals. They hide in tubes, play on wheels and build themselves nests.

Try this!

Make a finger puppet mouse

1. Find or make a cardboard tube that fits on your finger. Then cut out a head, some ears, whiskers and a tail.

2. Fold the head and glue it to the end of the tube. Add the ears, whiskers and curly tail.

3. Add some eyes and give your mouse a name.

Goldfish flash and gleam as they dart around the tank.

Woof!

Woof!

A basset hound's best-loved time is walking time!

Do you have a field to spare?

A Shetland pony is a very small horse, but a very big pet.

Safari adventure game

Help Lucy the lion cub to find her mother. The winner is the first person to reach her. Take it in turns to roll a die and move your buttons or markers around the board. You will need:

buttons or markers

die

START

1

2

3

4 Baby crocodile won't let you pass. Go back to start.

5

6

7

8 Wait for red panda to wake up and help you. Miss a go.

9

Sssssss!

10

Aroooo!

11 Wolf tells you about a short cut. Roll again.

12

13

14 Rainbow boa scares you. Go back five places.

Hold on tight!

18 Orang-utan gives you a lift. Move up two spaces.

19

20

21

17

Tsst! Tsst!

22 Water dragon stops to talk to you. Miss a go.

23

16

24

25

FINISH

15

26 Tortoise gives you a lift – the wrong way! Go back two spaces.

32

31

27

30 You chase two butterflies and get lost. Go back one space.

28

29

This edition is published by Armadillo,
an imprint of Anness Publishing Ltd,
108 Great Russell Street,
London WC1B 3NA;
info@anness.com

www.annesspublishing.com; twitter: @Anness_Books

Anness Publishing has a new picture agency outlet
for images for publishing, promotions or advertising.
Please visit our website www.practicalpictures.com
for more information.

A CIP catalogue record for this book
is available from the British Library.

Publisher: Joanna Lorenz
Senior Editor: Felicity Forster
Educational Consultant: Michael Chinery
Photography: John Freeman
Head Stylist: Melanie Williams
Designer: Mike Leaman Design Partners
Production Controller: Ben Worley

Manufacturer: Anness Publishing Ltd,
108 Great Russell Street, London WC1B 3NA, England
For Product Tracking go to: www.annesspublishing.com/tracking
Batch: 7186-23655-1127

PICTURE CREDITS
b=bottom, t=top, c=centre, l=left, r=right
ABPL: 21b;/Anness: Kim Taylor/Warren Photographic: 11tl, 11cbr,
13bl, 14ca, 15cra, 16cr, 17tl, 18bl,c,tr, 19tl;/Carol Cavanagh:
8br;/C. Hicks: 13cr;/Lucy Tizard: 10cbr, 26bl, 28tr, cra, clb, bl,
29tr;/Robert Pickett: 12c;/18tl, cl, bc, 19tl, 19tr, bl;/Jane Burton
26cl, 28crb;/Kit Houghton: 29b;/John Daniels: 29cr. Bruce Coleman
Limited: John Shaw: 4tl, 20cl;/Alain Compost: 4tr;/Stephen J.
Krasemann: 4bl;/Ingo Arndt: 4br;/Jane Burton: 5tl;/Gerald
Cubitt: 5br, 23bl;/Kim Taylor: 6tr; 7tl, 11tr, 13br, 19br, 23tr;/Hans
Reinhard: 6c;/Brian J Coates: 7tr;/Jeff Foott Productions: 7br, 8tr;/
Dr P. Evans: 9cr;/Mark Carwardine: 9bl;/Joe McDonald: 10t, 27tr;/
P. Kaya: 11cr;/Charles and Sandra Hood: 13cb;/Rod Williams:
5tl;/John Cancalosi: 16tr;/Alain Compost: 16tl;/Norman Owen
Tomalin: 16bl;/Christer Fredriksson: 16br;/Michael and Patricia
Fogden: 17cr;/Mary Plage: 17br;/Andy Purcell: 18cr;/Dr Frieder
Sauer: 19cl;/Jorg & Petra Wegner 20br, 27tl;/Andrew J. Purcell:
23br;/G. Ziesler: 24 t;/Charles and Sandra Hood: 25cl;/Pacific Stock:
25cr;/Fritz Prenzel: 26br;/Rod Williams: 27cl;/John Cancalosi:
27br;/Robert Maier: 28cla. FLPA: Michael Gore: 5c;/Fritz Polking:
5bl, 8bl, 9tr;/6br;/David Hosking: 8tl, 10b, 11b;/Ian Cartwright:
10car;/Lee Rue: 12tr;/Martin B. Withers: 14b, 15b, 23cr;/Michel
Gunther: 15tr, 28br;/John Tinning: 19ca;/D. Fleetham/Silvestris:
24c, 25br;/D. Perine/Sunset: 25t;/W. Wisniewski: 26tl;/Hugh Clark:
26tr;/Brake/Sunset:26cr;/E. & D. Hosking: 27cr;/Mark Newman:
27bl;/Terry Whittaker: 12tl, 17tr;/Michael and Patricia Fogden: 4c,
6tl, 13tr, 14bl, 15cra, 18br;/Natural Science Photos: M. W. Powles:
12b;/Oxford Scientific Films: 8c;/Steve Turner: 23tl;/Papilio
Photographic: 7cl, 6cr, 6bl , 11c, 14t, 14cr, 24bl, 24br, 25b;/Planet
Earth Pictures: Peter J. Oxford: 9cl;/James D. Watt: 9br;/Mary
Clay: 15cl;/Gary Bell:20tr;/Anup and Manoj Shah: 21tl;/M. & C.
Denis Huot: 21tr;/Ken Lucas: 22tr;/Mark Mattock: 22cl;/Edward
Coleman: 23cl;/Manoj Shah: 31br;/The Stock Market: 17bl;/
Zefa Pictures: 22bl.
    The publisher would like to thank the following children for
appearing in this book: Daisy, Faye, Grace, Philip, Tom, Zaafir.